CPSIA information can be obtained
at www.ICGtesting.com
Printed in the USA
LVHW080900260619
622385LV00019BA/1737/P

9 781072 864639